CAPE COD

CAPE COD

WILLIAM BERCHEN
and
MONICA DICKENS

A STUDIO BOOK · THE VIKING PRESS · NEW YORK

To Ursula for unending help   W B

To Roy   M

Text Copyright © 1972 by Monica Dickens
Photographs Copyright © 1972 by William P. Berchen
All rights reserved
First published in 1972 by The Viking Press, Inc.
625 Madison Avenue, New York, N.Y. 10022
Published simultaneously in Canada by
The Macmillan Company of Canada Limited
SBN 670-20322-x
Library of Congress catalog card number: 72-185985
Printed in U.S.A. by Neff Lithographing Co. Inc.
Bound by Montauk Book Mfg. Co. Inc.

Introduction

This is not a guidebook to Cape Cod, nor a eulogy for one of the loveliest places in America.

The words are about what Cape Cod looks like to someone who has lived here happily for twenty years.

The pictures are what Cape Cod looks like to the camera eye of a man's artistic vision.

The whole book represents what, for us, is the truth about Cape Cod, as we see it.

This land and the seas that surround it can be breathtakingly beautiful, at all seasons. We who live here have fallen in love with it. People who come to visit come back and back, for the same reason.

We are in love with Cape Cod.

But love, whatever Jessica believed, is not blind. True and lasting love sees clearly and honestly the good, the mediocre, and the bad. We are in love with what we know the Cape is like, not with a glorified travel brochure.

The Cape is pompously declared to be "God's country." Then why do we try to take it away from God?

Economic survival is said to depend on attracting tourists. But the more tourists, the less attractive the Cape, until eventually, perhaps, even the tourists won't want to come any more, having killed the thing they loved, and moved on like locusts to destroy some other place especially dear to God.

But the strange thing about the Cape is that even with the rape of places like Hyannis, Buzzards Bay, Provincetown, and Falmouth (which held out longer, but is now succumbing to the schizophrenia of luring customers by ruining the very things that lure them), even with all this, Cape Cod is still one the most magically beautiful places on earth.

Its beauty is endogenous. It is not enhanced by man. But neither has its essence been destroyed. Yet.

Monica Dickens
North Falmouth, Cape Cod

6

Sandy Neck, Barnstable ▶

What is Cape Cod?

It is the relic of the terminal moraine of a glacier, which dribbled down from Labrador six hundred thousand years ago and melted, leaving primeval boulders all over the western end, and a few lonely giants farther on.

It is a curve of sandbar, pitted with ponds, eaten into by tongues of sea. It is a loop of incomparable beaches, each one different, each one the answer to some unnamed desire.

Inland, it is a country of scrub oaks and meager pines, struggling to restore abandoned pastures to the forests the Indians knew before the salt plants cut the trees for fuel to boil down seawater. Village streets are tunnels of huge elms, in constant danger of being condemned by someone with a power saw.

A woman once chained herself to the trunk of an ancient Cape Cod tree, which had been declared diseased.

"Saw *me* in half, not this great tree that has guarded our house for generations."

But they sawed the chain in half, not her, and took her indoors, and a neighbor brought over the chocolate cake she always baked for bereavements.

The old houses are not built on the sandy ground. They grow from the firm

9

◄ Scorton Creek

roots of their cellars. They are painted white or Indian red, or weathered to the same color as the gray rocks and ancient vinegary apple trees.

There is no place on Cape Cod where you cannot smell the sea.

The weather is so fair that people have a fit if it rains for three days, but they wonder why the grass is not as green as England. A light mist is accused of being a fog. Frost comes so late that impatient children skate too early and fall through the ice. In hurricane time, the Weatherman, who "calls for" weather as if he could order it from a menu, reports the progress of tropical storms so frequently that everybody either gets so worked up that they are quite disappointed if the hurricane doesn't hit, or so bored that they make no preparations and lose their boats and garden furniture.

Winter snow is just heavy enough to bring the occasional magic of the dawn fire whistle blowing "No School." Summer windows go unscreened, so that flies can fly out as well as in. Lightning bugs dance indoors, while the people and their animals sit out under stars that stand amazed in a dark blue sky, staring at the beauty of the land.

If you live on the Cape, everybody you have ever known turns up sooner or later. Everyone wants to come to Cape Cod. When they do, they complain that it is ruined by too many people.

Total ruin is foiled by the beaches and by the great marshes, miles of bright, soggy green on which no developer can build. Everywhere else, bulldozers are into the scrub, and the pines that remain bear signs: "New Homes." "House Lots."

Every hundred yards along some mid-Cape roads, there is a grandiose entrance like a cemetery, with a lot of stonework and military geraniums and a chunk of simulated driftwood saying, "Clipper Ship Haven," "Ocean Hilands" (two miles from the shore and all land below sea level), "Old Mariners' Landing—2 and 3 bedroom Capes, Ranches, Splits, A-Frames."

Within, a network of tarred roads invades the undergrowth. Sometimes the developer runs out of money and goes away. Weeds begin to split the blacktop, and the sand dusts over it, and the stonework crumbles, and someone takes away the antiqued sign for firewood, and someone else has long ago stolen the geraniums and taken cuttings from them for the winter.

People who live in places like East Wareham or Plymouth pretend they live on the Cape, and they call their Chinese restaurants and used-car lots "Gateway to Cape Cod."

On the map, the shoulder of Cape Cod just might start at Plymouth or East Wareham, but since the Canal was broached in 1880 by five hundred Italians with shovels and wheelbarrows, everybody, including the car salesmen in East Wareham, knows that this is where the Cape begins.

Cape Cod is an island. This is part of the mystique. To get to an island, you must cross water, and there the magic starts.

The first road and rail crossings were by drawbridge. The new Canal was crowded with East Coast shipping, and by 1930 there was often a long line of cars through Buzzards Bay, waiting for the bridge to come down.

In 1935, when the new high bridges were finished, an optimistic Boston headline promised: NO MORE TRAFFIC JAMS TO CAPE COD. "Let it be hoped," the newspaper went on, "that new accessibility will not convert the quaint countryside into a shanty carnival."

The carnival came. The traffic jams remain.

"They should never have let it in," a Truro man said when the first car chugged slowly across the drawbridge in 1912. "It will be the end of Cape Cod."

The soaring road bridges are beautiful, exciting to drive over, tempting to jump from. More people jump from the Bourne bridge than from the Sagamore. No one knows why.

One lonely and confused man, who had been talked down by police and firemen many times from the parapet, eventually slipped and fell. "Suicide" is often an accident like this, a suicidal gesture that goes wrong and at this height must be fatal.

Another desperate man died during the drop, so that he did not breathe in any water and his body floated. When the Coast Guard pulled him out, every bone was broken, even the tiny hyoid.

No one has ever jumped from the railroad bridge, which is the most beautiful of all, an engineering masterpiece, more functional than it looks. Its towers are topped by cobwebbed mid-Victorian cones and shining steel balls that flash warnings to pilots, who occasionally ignore them and fly under the span.

It is the most beautiful railroad bridge in the world, and years ago, when the train was the best way to come to Cape Cod, a breathless symbol of promise to generations of summer children.

Buzzards Bay, and the bridge was down for *your* train, the precarious narrow track aiming for Monument Beach, Pocasset, Cataumet, North Falmouth, where a small crowd of cars and buggies waited to take you to the porch-and-turret paradise of Megansett.

When vandals burned the old North Falmouth station in 1969, they burned down a lot of people's sneakered past.

But the old childish nightmare remains, of a train trying to cross the Canal when the span is raised, and plunging into the water with shrieks, and babies thrown from windows.

When the trains ran regularly and the bridge went up and down five thousand times a year, the men who worked it knew when to expect the alert from Buzzards Bay that an approaching engine had tripped the signal. Now, with no passenger trains and the roadbed unsafe at more than twenty miles an hour, the occasional freight train runs in its own time. It may trip the signal, but there is only one man in the railroad station, and he may be answering the phone, helping a bus passenger, or taking a coffee break.

Perhaps one of the amiable men who make up the bridge crew is in the glass cabin in the tower, looking out at boats.

Look yonder—a train! And they lower the bridge.

13

◄ Ebb tide

But the bridge crew do many other things besides raise and lower the span and look out of the window. They grease the giant gears and sheaves. They climb up into the stainless steel balls to lift open a flap like a section of orange rind and replace a burned-out light bulb. They creep out on the top girders with a brush on the end of a broom handle to oil a cable that can't be reached any other way. They chip ice and snow and salt from the track seating at the bottom of the towers, and throw off beer cans and fishing floats that anglers leave on the rails.

So if no one has heard the signal or seen him coming, the engineer stops the train and gets out and calls up the bridge from the nearest drugstore.

The machinery of the vertical lift bridge is at the top of each tower. A coffin-size elevator runs up one side. When it won't run, there is a steel ladder, raked by the breezes from Stony Point. To get to the machinery on the other side, you walk out along the raised track, past the experimental NASA device that will one day enable a satellite to transmit unsporting news about where the fish are.

Look up. Above the network of girders, the steel cones hoist the shining balls to reel around the tilting sky. Look down. The swift tidal water rushes far below. The towers rush down in a dwindling perspective of vertigo. Safer to stare out at the Canal entrance by Hog Island, or across at the peaceful houses of Gray Gables, where Grover Cleveland had his summer White House.

It was Cleveland who first made the Cape *the* place to summer; hence all those marvelous great shingled houses around Buzzards Bay, once run by half a dozen imported servants, now by salty, browned grandmothers who don't make a fuss about sand.

Look yonder! Down the side of the Canal from Sagamore comes a toy engine with one freight car and a caboose. You can either ride down on the span or take the elevator to the bottom of the tower and stand underneath as the counterweight rises and the track comes down to lock neatly into place. Just before it lands, the sight-seeing boat they call the *Onset Howler* nips underneath for thrills, loud-speaker howling, passengers ducking and squealing.

14

The train rattles by. The span goes up again. The heavy counterweights sink down and stop just short of your head. The boats that have been held up by the Canal dispatcher at the Canal entrance begin to pass under the bridge. The high span rides the sky between the beautiful towers.

It can be seen from all the high land of the Upper Cape, wheeling and turning, never where you expect it, since the Canal runs, not north and south, but east and west, which even people who have lived on the right side of it all their lives don't always know.

There are no tolls now, but in the days of the old Eastern Steamship Line, when the steamers *Boston* and *New York* ran between those cities, it used to cost them fifteen hundred dollars for a round trip through the canal. Every evening, crowds lined the banks to see the lighted boat pass through to its own music, and a thirteen-year-old trumpeter stood on a lawn at Gray Gables and blew his heart out into "Taps."

New York families summering on the Lower Cape used to take the boat through the Canal to Boston, and another to Provincetown, and the train to Truro or Wellfleet or Chatham.

When the railroad ran through to Provincetown in 1870, before the highway, it changed the pattern of life on Cape Cod. People began to make money out of tourists. The salt plants at Truro and Falmouth went out of business, because fish could now travel fresh in ice on the trains. Fishermen prospered for a while, but the industry was already dying. The silting harbors were too small for the bigger boats that fished the farther banks. The loss of life at sea was too great. In 1841, more than eighty-seven men died in a single night of storm, and at one time there were more than a hundred widows in the small town of Truro.

Cape Cod is still a land of many widows. A couple retires here, and the man, worn out by making enough money to retire to Cape Cod, dies shoveling snow or digging a little corn patch. His widow battles on with this fine new life they planned

15

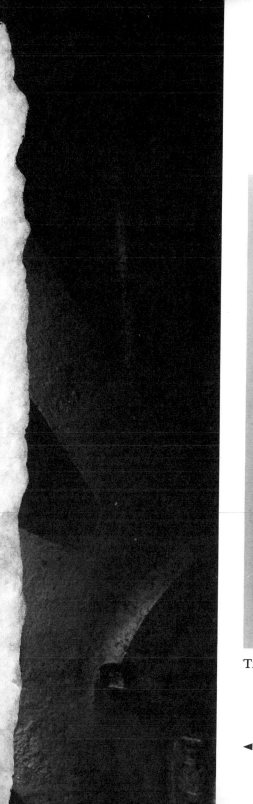

The bridgekeeper

◄ Giant gearwheel of the railroad bridge over Buzzards Bay

together, or takes to good works, or the League of Women Voters, or sherry, which is more respectable than gin.

One of the difficulties about living and working on the Cape all year is that leisured visitors, both the invited ones and those who drive three thousand miles and surprise you with a call from the corner store, expect you to be at leisure too, permanently, from guest to guest.

They see the whole Cape as a perpetual vacation place, carefree, prosperous, smiling as it greets them with raised prices.

They don't see the backside of Cape Cod. The backside used to mean Nauset Beach. Now it means the poor.

There are several schools of thought about the poor who are scattered all over Cape Cod.

One is that it is better to be poor here, because you are surrounded by free amenities, like the weather and the beaches.

Another is that it is worse, because you are surrounded by people who have more money and nicer houses than you.

There is another which thinks that poverty is a permanent state, like the color of your skin. Labeled Poor, you will always need help, and there will always be jobs for those who help you.

Another, while agreeing that in any society there will always be some people who can't ever cope, believes that most poverty need only be a stage on the way up to something better. You should be helped to get off the backside, not to stay there.

Another sees the Cape's poor like drug addicts and discharged mental patients: sure, they need help and housing, but not next door to me.

For years and years the pattern of life on the backside of Cape Cod has been to pay a cheap winter rent and move in with Grandma or Aunt Rose when the rents double or triple in June and the summer tenants trot willingly to the fleecing.

Some displaced people had to camp out. Some families had to live in trucks and old cars, and wash their hair in ponds and kneel on the car floor to dry it by the heater. They could not leave the Cape, since they had no money and nowhere to go. They could not find a cheap place here to settle in and look for work.

They could not find work anyway, because there were no unskilled winter jobs, except after snowstorms, and even the lowliest summer jobs were snapped up by eager young college boys and girls who were bright and attractive. And white.

Gradually the backside people, even those who had got used to moving in with Grandma and Aunt Rose, thirteen people in half a house, began to see that all this was unfair.

But it is the pattern of life, said the Cape Codders (which used to mean anyone who was monosyllabically surly enough to be a quaint native, and now means anyone who has been here long enough to root a wisteria). We all live that way.

How about split families, they said, with the husband sweltering in New York and the family on the Cape? How about the children who for generations have summered with the salty browned sailing grandmothers? And the sons of scientists who move out of cheap Woods Hole housing to spend the summer with a girl on a derelict boat in the harbor? Is all that unfair?

Grandma and Aunt Rose didn't say much. They were pretty busy. The frontside grandparents complained at cocktail parties on oceanside lawns that the only people the summer pattern was unfair to was them.

"I can't do a thing next week. I've got my grandchildren coming." (Eyes to heaven.)

"Last year you were disappointed because they all went to Colorado. I thought that was why you retired to the Cape—so that your married children could come back with *their* children."

"I didn't know they'd come back with children like that. They never go to bed. They eat all the peanuts when people come for drinks."

Meanwhile, some of the poor were waking from their long nomadic apathy.

19

Farm stand, Route 6A

East Dennis

They dug into cottages and motel rooms. They learned how to bully civil servants. They read leaflets that advised "disruption, harassment, and increased militancy."

Advertisements appeared in city newspapers warning tourists not to come to Cape Cod and drive the natives into the street. This made anyone who had looked forward to renting a summer cottage very nervous, especially if they had paid a deposit.

Before Memorial Day, other advertisements invited sympathizers to "Come on down and do anything you like on the bridges."

This did not mean chucking yourself off, but joining an amiable march of displaced tenants across the Canal, carrying babies and slogans, while motorists yelled out of the window, "Get yourself a job!" and the marchers made rude signs at them with their fingers.

Policemen from all over the Cape turned up in crowd control regalia of helmet and shield and gas mask. In case of car blockades, garage owners were paid to park their tow trucks all day by the bridges. Everyone had quite a good time. The Governor of Massachusetts took note.

While he was taking it, several homeless families took over the National Guard Armory in Hyannis. The noise of babies wailing and children shrieking was like the echoes of hell under the vaulted gymnasium roof. Bored and bitter teen-agers, with nothing to do and no heart or will to find anything, lay out the heat of noon on army cots. Mothers took turns making soups and stews. A woman with rollers in her hair ate a steak without putting in her teeth, and embarrassed a boyish local reporter by accusing him of trying to make money out of the poor.

One delicate young mother, very near to giving birth, worried about what would happen to her six other small children when she went to the hospital.

And wept out of big eyes like plums because the pattern of the Cape was changing again, more violently, and there would be fewer cheap places to rent next winter.

"I'm not risking another sit-in."

Over at Dunroamin' by a lake in the woods, the Portuguese owner, who had

24

built the cabins and the pool himself, wept with rage as he tried to repair the winter's damage in time to get his summer customers in. Shrubs torn out. Rocks in the swimming pool. Holes kicked in the cabin walls. Human and animal excrement ground into the carpets.

"This Cape is changing. The kids look at a landlord the way they look at a cop. The women yell four-letter words at me when I tell them their lease is up. For a Portugee, that's hard to take, from a woman. I'm shutting up next winter. Getting off the Cape. It does not enthuse me."

A black father of three got sick of looking for work and spent some of his welfare allowance on booze. Thus proving to the delight of his neighbor that what he had been saying in the bars was right. Welfare recipients spend the money on booze and are unemployed only because they don't want to work.

Later the black man was arrested for falling down in the street, and locked up with some youths who were caught sleeping on the beach. Thus proving that to be poor on Cape Cod can be a crime. Shove it under the rug, as the Pilgrims in that first year at Plimoth shoved their sick onto an island and forgot them.

As chickens will peck a diseased hen to death. As horses will kick a feeble old mare in the head, so she can't hold back the herd.

The neighbor, who was also the landlord, managed to get rid of the nuisance of the black family, with their broken tricycles and unattractive laundry lines. That summer, he took in a Fresh Air kid, who had been dragged to the Cape to make up the quota, and spent the two weeks complaining that the ocean was not as much fun as the neighborhood pool in the Bronx.

In a lopsided gray cottage near a bog ripening with tiny young cranberries, a slightly senile old lady was quietly starving to death, because she had been warned by an aggressive woman who saw her exchanging food stamps in the supermarket, that if she stayed on Welfare, she must come to protest meetings and learn to hate the people who doled out the money.

On the shores of a wide bay, a city family was sanding the bottom of their boat and dusting out a house full of last summer's shells and unfinished jigsaws.

As she swept the porch and looked out at the sea beyond the humpy dunes, and the familiar shapes of green marsh in the river, the mother's eyes were calm with relief at the unchanging safety of Cape Cod.

The eager young boys and girls come from all over the United States and Europe to work here. They need the money for colleges and cars. They also want to spend the summer on this sandy Mecca of the young. East of the Rockies, half the pieces of shirt cardboard held up by hitchhikers say: CAPE COD.

They work in shops and garages and snack bars. They warble songs from old musicals as they carry trays of cocktails. They punch cash registers in supermarkets. They make salads in inferno restaurant kitchens, endlessly filling little plastic bowls with one ring of red onion, one of green pepper, one sculpted radish, half a tomato, and the outside leaves of what was used for Hearts of Lettuce.

Bearded sons of talcumed executives work on the roads and garbage trucks. Beautiful and brilliant college sophomores, who have never lifted a finger in their mother's house, scrub out cabins, sanitize motel bathrooms "for your protection," and change dirty linen.

Every morning on a wide curving beach on Vineyard Sound, a husky young lifeguard drills a squad of middle-aged ladies who want to get into last year's swim suit. He watches the sea for foolhardy swimmers. He knows half a dozen ways to save a life.

These lifeguards, perched like Rodin figures on their lookout thrones, or patrolling the prostrate toasted flesh with a gorilla plod through the soft sand, arouse hysterical interest in very young girls. Girls of their own age usually come to the beach with a boy who does not have to watch the sea all the time.

There are not enough jobs for all the young people who want to summer on the Cape. A Help Wanted advertisement may bring a hundred breathless applicants.

26

Time out ▶

Restaurants and hotels hire too many, in case some don't turn up. If they all come, some of them find they have no job. Rooms and food are expensive. Until August, when some people get sick of working, even dishwashing is impossible to find. The only employers who are interested are pimps. There is a certain car park in Hyannis where a fresh young college or high-school girl may be bought for the price of a meal or a bed.

They can get emergency food vouchers from the Welfare Office, but if they are under twenty-one, their parents must be called.

"I'm calling from Provincetown, on Cape Cod. We have your daughter here. She seems to be without funds."

The telephone explodes. The Welfare worker jerks it away from her ear and raises an eyebrow at the sullen young face drooping by her desk.

"Did you tell him he was militaristic and should have been sterilized before he could have children?"

"Maybe." The curtains of hair close over the face.

"That's your Dad then."

Provincetown, at once the most sophisticated and most wild place on the Cape, is where the drifters drift to and pile up. In other towns they stay for a while and drift on. In Provincetown they stay for months and even years, sharing a dilapidated house, spreading venereal disease and hepatitis, caught up in the *laissez-faire* mystique of this ravaged little fishing village.

To those who remember Provincetown when you could hear the boots of the fishermen clumping home on the board sidewalk at evening, the garish mêlée of tawdry shops in weathered house fronts, and old barns and sail lofts crammed with junk art, is nothing less than tragedy.

They never go there any more. Everyone else goes there, from the freakiest weirdo to the squarest tourist in Bermuda shorts and black shoes and knee socks.

The only thing that can be said for the spectacle of Provincetown is that it

29

◄ View of Sandwich from Bailey's Island

Gingerbread house in Cotuit

Out buildings, Chatham

draws people away from the rest of the Cape. Even the homosexuals don't stop until they teeter on this outer edge of the Atlantic. There is one end of a certain beach near the tip where any golden summer girl can walk a quarter of a mile along the crowded strand without being noticed.

Some of the golden Cape Cod girls get jobs as waitresses at expensive restaurants, at a starvation wage, plus tips which they share, unwillingly, with the bus boys.

Sometimes they have to rush out after a slightly boozed customer and say, "Don't you realize I only get ninety-six cents an hour?"

Or a more subtle approach: "Was the food good?"

"Oh, sure, sure . . . what did we have? . . . Sure."

"Was the service good?"

"Oh, sure, honey. Just fine."

"Well"—the waitress shoves down a quick vision of her proud New England mother—"your tip didn't show it."

Tipsily he fishes out a crumpled dollar bill—"Keep the change"—and weaves out to his car to add to the hazards of the road.

Into such a restaurant one night come Eric and Eleanor Boomhower, a newly married couple from a small town in Iowa. They know it will cost them the earth, but what the hell. They aren't going to take any traveler's checks home.

The restaurant is famous. A Gourmet's Paradise. They keep hearing about it on the local radio station. Shall we? They're a bit sick of clam rolls and pizza. Why not? She puts on the aqua pants suit and he puts on the orange jacket that she still thinks may be a bit too loud, and they drive to the restaurant, where a merry boy in a striped fisherman's sweater drives their car away to the end of a vast, filled car park.

Inside the paradise there are candlelit bars, sophisticated drinkers, three boys and a guitar, waitresses whose uniforms reach the crotch, flickering lamps to tone down even the orange jacket. The Boomhowers join the end of a long line of men

Wellfleet, near the harbor

House in Chatham

Bass River

Sandwich burial ground

◄ Salt meadow, Cape Cod National Seashore

Plume grass

Salt Spray roses ►

Nauset Beach

Marsh bridgewalk at Yarmouth Port

Farm pond in West Falmouth

Inlet, East Falmouth

Wild berries along a pond in Barnstable

◄ Pine forest in the National Seashore reserve

Bayside cottage in Chatham

and women with hairpieces and wigs to cover sea-ruined hair. After about twenty minutes they arrive before a jolly young man in a Turkish blouse who gives them a number, like the draft, or the old days at the butcher's counter.

"Won't you enjoy one of our cocktail lounges until your table is ready?"

"My wife and I don't usually—"

An order is an order, however jolly. They go into the Olde Englyshe Tappe Roome and sit in chairs made out of half barrels, with a plate of crackers and cheese on the barrel top between them. Can you get a Coke in here? Would that be Englyshe enough? The waitress doesn't come anyway. Eric Boomhower eats an enormous amount of crackers and cheese to cover the fact that he is trying to get her eye, in case he never gets it.

He does. Her suntanned smile beams over him. Her huge thighs menace him at eye level.

"Two sweet Manhattans," he manages to say, and notices at that moment that everyone else in the Tappe Roome seems to be drinking martinis.

The Manhattans are so long in coming that they have eaten the rest of the cheese and crackers and don't really want any dinner. Can they creep out without the waitress or the jolly young man seeing them? What will the merry fellow in the car park think? Could they find their car without him?

He's got the key.

Just as they are getting up their nerve to run for it, the Manhattans arrive. As they are taking their first sip, an amplified voice calls something that sounds like "The Bloomflower party."

They jump and look around. Who on earth—? Oh, us. The waitress is there. "You may carry in your drinks." But she is there with a bill, and so Mr. Boomhower has to put down his glass and find his wallet and wait for the change and figure out the tip before he and his Manhattan can follow Mrs. Boomhower, who is following a hostess through room after room of people eating or staring over paper lobster bibs.

49

They come to port in the last room at the last table, in a dark corner by a window with a view of the car park. Perhaps they will see their car. They look at the menu. Eleanor couldn't get her contact lenses in after swimming, which is just as well since she cannot see the prices. What can they order that won't be much more than they want? They see other people's plates going by. The filet mignon looks like porterhouse, and the roast beef is cut as thick as a two-by-four.

They finish their Manhattans and drink three glasses of chlorinated water, which an obliging young man in a long stained apron tied twice around his coltish waist keeps filling up. They decide to order Fisherman's Platter, because people back home are going to want them to have had Cape Coddy things.

Their waitress, labeled Mary-Lu, is plump and harried, tendrils of damp hair on her hot face. But her smile is indomitable, and Mrs. Boomhower confides that she has a bird's appetite, and may she have a child's portion?

"I'm sorry. Baked, French fried, hashed brown, or Delmonico."

"No potatoes, thank you."

"Baked squash, green beans, cauliflower o grattin, Harvard beets."

"We don't care for any vegetables. Just the Fisherman's Platter and salad."

"Would you care for another cocktail?" She picks up the Manhattan glasses, only one of which has a cherry stem. Mr. Boomhower has eaten the other. After the *faux pas* of the child's plate, she won't be surprised to find them a one-drink couple.

She brings the salads an hour before anything else, and some sticky sweet rolls, with not enough butter. ("*Ask her for some more, Eric.*") But Mary-Lu looks so rushed and flustered, carrying enormous trays of food and getting her ample waist grabbed by a four-drink man at an aisle table, that they haven't the heart to bother her.

When their platters come, they are intimidatingly oval, to accommodate half a lobster, an ear of corn, a square chunk of breaded haddock, three codfish balls, two shrimps stuffed with bread, clams stuffed with God knows what, a paper cup of tartar sauce, a plastic dish of oily butter, and a mound of French fries.

51

◄ Country store in Brewster

"We didn't—" But Mary-Lu, inexorable as the Fates, dots the table with a half dozen dishes of cold vegetables *au jus* (in their own cooking water).

The butter makes a terrible mess on the Boomhowers and the tablecloth. There are no corn holders, or crackers or picks for the lobster, so they wash their fingers in the water glasses. Eric eats in silence. Eleanor casts around for things to talk about. She sees the mute couples all around them, and panics. Is this what marriage is?

At the next table misguided parents have brought two small boys who whine and make faces like apes and waste enormous amounts of Blue Ribbon Charbroil Steak and dash in and out to the men's room because there is a hot-air hand drier in there.

When the Boomhowers get their bill, it is about half what they usually spend on food in a week. If they give a two-dollar tip, that will be it, until they can cash another traveler's check. But poor Mary-Lu seems so harassed. They'd better. They leave the money on the table and walk out, so as not to inflict on her the embarrassment of thanks. As they reach the doorway, she runs after them with her brief apron and damp tendrils flying.

"Don't you know I only get ninety-six cents an hour?"

The next day Mrs. Boomhower goes to a hardware store and buys an electric coffeepot to heat soup in their motel room. Eric sends his mother a postcard with a picture of the famous restaurant.

We ate here last nite. Wow.

There are a million different ways to pick up a bit of cash in the summer on Cape Cod.

You can row a garbage boat around the big yachts in the crowded harbors, and meditate on the money tied up there.

52

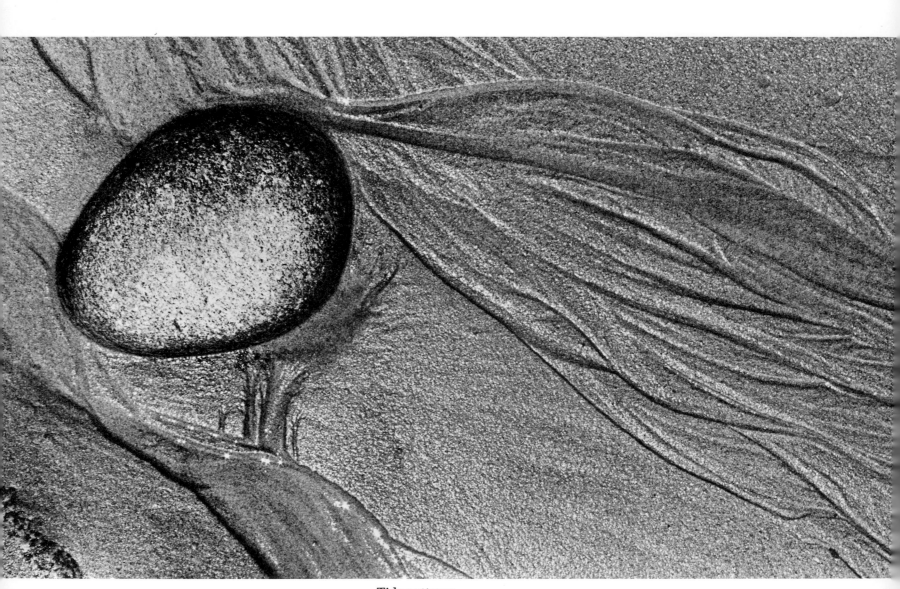

Tide patterns

You can drive an ice-cream wagon. You can paint or sculpt or make pottery, five plates to a set to show you don't cater to middle-class paired dinners, and peddle it on the sidewalk at Provincetown or Woods Hole.

You can sweep in as a star to one of the summer theaters at a salary of three thousand a week, and bully the apprentices, playing big fish in a little pond. You can be a theater usher and see all the stars for nothing, with your hair glossed down your back for patrons to admire as they wait for you to flush out the wrong people you have put into their seats.

You can try for a prize of seven hundred dollars in a Rocking Chair Marathon, rocking day and night among rivals loaded to the eyeballs with amphetamines, your chair donated to the Smithsonian if you win.

You can sell bottles of Chatham Bluff air, or Buzzards Bay seawater to cook lobsters in. You can set out a bunch of rusty keys and one rowlock and some bent saucepan lids and a souvenir plate of Kennedy's funeral in your garden shed and call it Antiques.

You can run a gift shop or a motel.

There is this lady who owns the Laughing Lobster Gifts and Cards in a mid-Cape town. People steal things all the time, especially in wet weather when the shop is full. So she rigged up a half-open pocketbook on a back counter, with a wallet showing, wired to an alarm.

The wallet was taken several times, with a dollar in it, but the only time the alarm went off was when a new assistant considerately closed the bag.

Bells went off all over the shop. A family who was browsing for a gift for the dog-sitter dropped a piece of Copenhagen china and ran out, thinking it was a fire. A young winter schoolteacher in summer policeman's uniform ran in and arrested the new assistant. In the excitement a pair of gold earrings disappeared, and an ashtray with a comic picture of a child drowning in a cranberry bog.

To run a motel on Cape Cod is one of the things that people promise them-

Provincetown Beach

◄ Provincetown

selves they will do when they retire. Many of them have done it, but there is still room to squeeze in a few more.

It can be profitable, but every year fewer people can afford the high prices, and more tents and camping trailers roll across the bridges.

And you can't just build a motel and decorate it and furnish it. You have to keep redecorating and refurnishing. Even rebuilding it, when Number 22 forgets his key and shoulders down the door at 3 A.M. rather than wake the management.

Summer people make almost as much mess as the winter tenants of Dunroamin. They also steal light bulbs and tissues (and ask for more), towels, blankets, pillows, and anything else removable, even the color television.

Families arrive exhausted and quarrelsome. Menopausal women crash into the room and tear the bed apart to complain about it. The only people who don't quibble about the price are the men who come in with someone else's wife.

She always waits in the car. The motel keeper can see her out of the office window, checking her makeup in the rear-view mirror.

"A double room."

"For you and your wife?"

"Er—yes." He registers as John So-and-so.

"Mr. and Mrs. So-and-so?"

"Er—yes."

"Please register your wife." Thus framing him into violating the True Name Law, as well as someone else's wife.

The manless mothers at Dunroamin had better luck than that. The owner had to allow night visitors, because someone at the Welfare department told him that they didn't want a bunch of frustrated women on their hands.

Unless it's a family, more than one couple can't share a motel room, so one pair books and another sneaks in. Sometimes several.

The lady who runs the Gitche Goomee Motor Haven, somewhere along the nightmare tripper strip of West Yarmouth, heard a turmoil in the night and knocked

59

◄ Lobsterman, West Falmouth

on the door of Number 14. There were about twenty people in the room, spilling liquor on the chairs and the carpet and the beds.

"Glad you came," said the man who opened the door. "Save us the trouble of calling you to complain that the mattresses are damp."

In a huge hotel on a sparkling beach, Mrs. Doris Fein sits in the dim lobby wearing sunglasses and a nylon petaled bonnet over the hairdo she will never take into the sea, and all the jewelry Mr. Fein gave her before she lost him, because she dares not leave it in the room with all those undergraduate chambermaids around.

There is nothing to do, except swimming, sunning, sailing, riding, sight-seeing, bridge, tennis, golf, shuffleboard, relaxing. She does not feel comfortable relaxing. She is here because an advertisement for this hotel, with "Milton Shapiro, Manager," was a coded way to tell her that it was safe to come here, although the manager's name is really Tim O'Leary. Mr.Fein tried to rent a summer house once, in the wrong place on Cape Cod.

"Feeling better?" A man she met last night when she was moaning at the bar comes by in madras shorts, strutting on his heels, hands in tight pockets, bottom oscillating.

"Since I didn't eat today. They should never served me that crazy lobster."

That crazy lobster may have been caught by an Episcopal clergyman, who has four hundred lobster traps down in Buzzards Bay, cartographically the armpit of Cape Cod.

Most mornings from May to November you can see him chugging his little green lobster boat out of the harbor, Nordic and serene, more at home in the bare wheelhouse of the *Hunter* with the shifting sea ahead, than in the pulpit of St. Margaret's, facing the bland, committed faces.

He exchanges salutes with waking yachtsmen. He does not wave to powerboats. Propellers cut lobster lines, and a lost trap costs ten dollars.

Out in the bay dozens of different-colored floats are bobbing in groups above

60

the fruitful rock ledges below. Later, when the breeze whips up the whitecaps, it is harder to see the floats, which is why lobstermen go out so early.

There are too many lobster traps all around Cape Cod. A commercial license costs a hundred dollars a year, but that can be made in two good days. Many retired men have a fling at it. The old-time fishermen, whose families have been lobstering for generations, pull up the new traps, take what is in them, put the float inside, and let the concrete sinker take them down. A newcomer has to wait them out until they leave him alone. Then he, too, begins to find himself incensed when he sees alien floats over the rocky places he discovered, and is tempted to sink those traps himself. That's when he knows he is a lobsterman.

From the bay on a promising blue morning the houses on the shores and headlands emerge from the drifts of mist to begin their day in the sun. Cars shuttle on the highway along the inland ridge. A woman with long blowing hair runs with a leaping dog on a curve of white beach. An early sailboat flaps at the pier of an old gray house whose porches are windows to the sea.

The *Hunter* cuts through a small green swell, trailing a cloud from the black stovepipe that is her funnel. At the first cluster of green-and-white floats, her captain idles the engine, hooks in the line, and turns it around the winch. The trap comes up over the side, dripping eel grass. Inside are two big conch shells, a mêlée of spider crabs, and two smallish lobsters. One of them has one normal claw with its cutter and crusher, and one embryonic one. Lobsters shed bits of themselves or get eaten by each other, but they can grow replacements.

The captain measures the lobsters from eye socket to the edge of the carapace and throws one back into the sea. He bands the claws of the other and puts it in the holding tank, takes the spider crabs out of the trap with an ingenious device manufactured by his eight-year-old son—a nail in the end of a stick—baits the trap with flounder carcasses, and chucks it overboard, and the *Hunter* chugs on to the next green-and-white float.

Her working days are numbered. The independent lobsterman, both the new

62

and the old hand, will eventually be edged out of the sea by huge factory ships, pulling thousands of traps and freezing and canning lobsters on board.

Good-by to the freedom of solitude. On a boat like the *Hunter* there is not enough work for two men, and why split the profits? Most lobster fishermen fathom the secret morning seas alone.

Hence the expression "lonely as a lobsterman."

This is what it is like to live on Cape Cod, and fall in love with it.

You can do what you like. Nobody bothers you. You can go to a party every night, or never at all. You can live in a village where the shabbiest house is beautiful because of what the sea weather has done to the wood, and where there are a dozen different class levels, and the only way you know which one is yours is that if you invite someone from above or below, they won't invite you back.

You can live in a town with sewers and traffic lights and Colonial gas stations. You can live in a one-room cabin on the outer dunes, or the elemental edge of Sandy Neck where the Great Marshes nurture the source of life, and sea and sky and broad wet sands merge into one.

In winter you can skate on a different pond for every day of the year. Snow on the mainland side of the Canal is often rain on the other. You can ride a horse all winter on wooded trails and deserted beaches, hoofs drumming the sand, racing the gulls through the blown spume.

You can live in the freedom of Woods Hole as a scientist or a layabout, accepted in your uniform of beard and patched blue jeans, as long as you have something to say.

You can attend a Town Meeting and listen to a two-hour debate on whether Mr. Cardoza should move his front fence three yards back to accommodate a drainpipe. Those on the right back the pipe-layers. Those on the left back Cardoza (who is

Marsh, Province Land Reservation ▶

Along Chatham inlet

Winter on Cape Cod Bay

Salt Pond, Eastham

Shawme Lake, Sandwich ▶

Beached boats in Scudder Lane, Barnstable

◄ Old King's Highway, West Dennis

Old King's Highway, on the way to the Cape

Phragmites grass

Wellfleet

Snow-covered fields in Sandwich ▶

Sandy Neck, Barnstable Beach

Dunes at Sandy Neck

Mud Cove, Pocasset

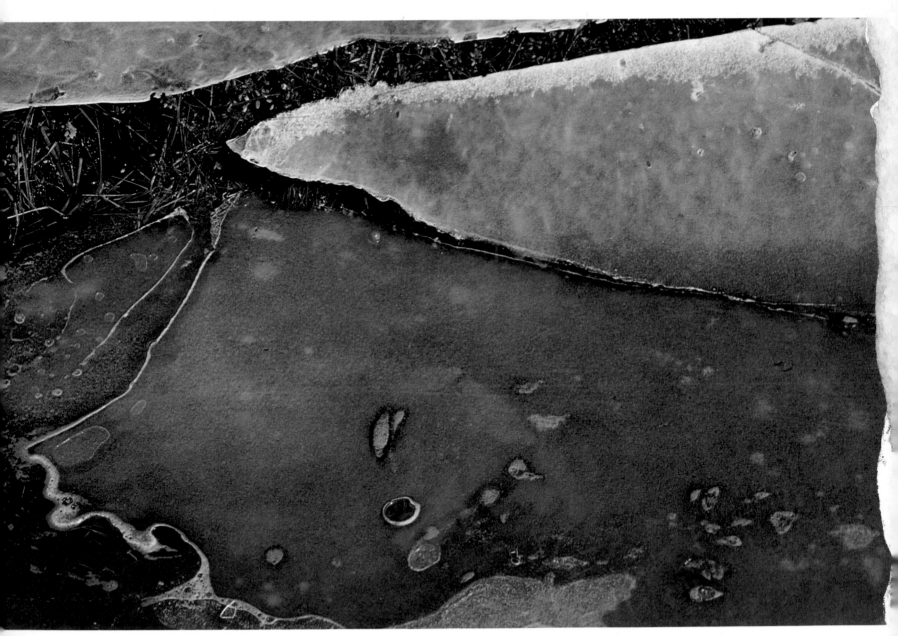

Cranberry bog

related to most of them). The rest of the perennial opinionists back anyone's right to do anything, with a certain amount of confusion and a great deal of impassioned oratory.

The Moderator lets people ramble on, to preserve the rural flavor and to keep suburban experts and legal mouthpieces out of this traditional debate, which has maintained the Cape, battered but with its soul intact.

Since the days when it was an all-day spree, with the women serving coffee and Town Meeting cake, the sole embargo is that opponents may insult each other only through the Chair. If you have to say, "Mr. Moderator, that's a stinking lie," it dulls the edge of the abuse.

You can go to an A.A. meeting anywhere, any night of the week. There are more alcoholics on Cape Cod than in the South End of Boston. The old drink from loneliness, the young from boredom and because there are enough thick grown-ups who will go into a liquor store for them. The middle years have their Working Drunks. They can pass out every night and still somehow get through the day on the job, leaning back when they have to talk to someone.

You can grow roses and azaleas and tomatoes as big as a baseball. You can abandon your pets at the end of the vacation: kittens in a grocery bag, puppies in a carton, left at the side of Route 6, or even on it, to be hit.

You can cross the Sandwich marsh on the boardwalk which, when it is not being vandalized by irresponsibles, supports never less than two responsible small boys with rod and line. Three who have caught a very small flounder have tied a string to the hook and hung him from the bridge, "so he can swim around." The boardwalker asks if that isn't cruel. "Na, he's used to it." Do they catch him every day?

In summer you can walk along the side of the highway and pick up the unspeakable things that people throw from cars. If you live near a road, you can pick them out of your front garden, while the slower drivers cruising around to see the old houses will note you as a feature of the rustic scene.

You can dance naked on Brush Hollow Beach at Truro, or revitalize your spirit in the charging surf of Nauset, or ride the dunes in a buggy with elephantine wheels, which may kill the holding grass and leave a hollow that will be there in ten years' time.

You can put up your tent among the pines and live like a liberated king. Or park your shining curtained trailer in a campsite and set out the witch balls and plaster gnomes and tack up a wrought-iron sign with your name, so that other campers can visit you, just like home.

You can go to a pow-wow at Mashpee, where the Wampanoag tribe strives to remain intact and separate from the society that once forced them into a reservation here.

The children hop and wriggle through Indian dances, and the famous fireball game ends the show. A huge ball of tightly packed rags soaked in kerosene is set alight and kicked over an open field by hundreds of excited feet. It flares as it rolls, and the skittering brown legs flicker and jump in flame and shadow, as if they were part of the fire. A boy scoops up the ball with a shriek and throws it. A wild girl kicks it under a car. Will the car blow up? A hero of fourteen crawls after it, and tosses the flaming mass into the crowd, who scream and run and wrestle with each other in an exhilaration that rampages all night.

You can watch the young Campus Crusaders for Christ parading the main street of Hyannis to the tune of a soft drink commercial:

'You-ouve gotta lot to live, and Jesus gotta lot to gi-ive . . .'

Follow them to the hall and sing innocent clapping ditties and listen to a boy with a guitar intoning songs that ask questions, *"Who am I? Where am I going?"* but give no answers, and hear some of the devouts give testimony of their faith. By day the boys wash dishes and cook in a chain restaurant where a chart in the kitchen tells them the company's way to ruin good food, but they are in love with life and can survive.

82

You can attend a writers' conference, with a new-grown beard and a pipe and a sheaf of manuscript under your tweedy arm. A fellow student who is having some difficulty getting her lips over her long teeth asks you, "Are you published?"

"No." The whiskers hide the blush.

"Oh, goody. Neither am I."

If the island flavor of Cape Cod draws people hypnotically across the Canal, the sign, "To the Islands" is irresistible. They must step off again to the enchanted islands of Martha's Vineyard and Nantucket.

Away with systems! Away with a corrupt world! Let us breathe the air of the enchanted island.

Golden lie the meadows; golden run the streams; red gold is on the pine stems. The sun is coming down to earth, and walks the fields and waters.

The sun is coming down to earth, and the fields and the waters shout to him golden shouts.

Every weekend from May to September, a lady in square flowered pants brings a busload of seekers from New York. They go to Martha's Vineyard, and then they go home exhausted, wondering where the enchantment went.

The golden meadows are there, and the sun on the fields and waters, but the day trippers don't see much more than Vineyard Haven and Oak Bluffs and the inside of a bus to Gay Head, where the fog is down over the colored cliffs and the Indians have zippers in their costumes.

The man who runs the snack bar on one of the ferryboats listens to their excited talk on the way over. "Boy, I can't wait to take in that island."

On the way back the same guy drags himself to the counter for a beer. "So what's so great about Martha's Vineyard?"

The snack bar man doesn't tell him. Nobody who loves the Vineyard does. They keep the secret to themselves.

On the way to the island, he sells expensive sandwiches to small discontented children, who take one bite and throw the rest to the gulls that glide back and forth all day over this seagoing cornucopia.

Two pubescent girls with braids come to the bar and ask for coffee. One of them puts her floppy shoulder bag on the counter, over the plastic cup that is left out for tips. At the far end, the other fusses over her coffee and spills it. While the man is wiping up, the other girl swoops bag and tip cup off the counter and disappears.

The boat is docking. Everybody has thronged to the companionway in a mad crush to be off first, and the braided girl with the shoulder bag is lost in the crowd.

Brown boys like South Sea urchins swim off the starboard side to dive for coins. Below the pier a huddle of tiny children beg from the shallows. The people waiting to embark have spent so much anyway that they toss down their few pieces of change. The children scrabble in the water like hens after corn, then stand again, teeth chattering, with their chant like the cries of old London:

How 'bout a quar-ter?

84

Beach plum ▶

◀ Dexter Grist Mill on Shawme Lake

Gravestone carving

There is another island called Monomoy, which hangs down below Chatham like a troubadour's sleeve on the elbow of Cape Cod. No ferryboats run there, and soon nobody will be allowed to walk on it at all. The lighthouse and four bleached houses will be pulled down, and the long sandy wilderness left to the birds.

Until then, the Audubon Society still runs a small boat from Chatham for bird watchers and others who tag along because it is the only way to get to Monomoy.

They meet at Chatham Bluff: a dedicated young guide who can identify six hundred North American birds, a druggist and his wife from Indianapolis, a fanatical Canadian birder who goes all over the United States checking off his Life List, which is birds you must see before you die, and two women who just want to go to Monomoy.

The captain of the boat looks like that sailor king, George V. He takes them through the harbor mist, past the sand bar where a line of boats is anchored for clamming, and stops off a shallow beach. The motley little party wades ashore, carrying lunches and binoculars and shoes. King George V backs off, and they are alone in the fog on Monomoy.

They take the old truck down the outer beach, where clouds of gulls rise up before them and drop down again behind. The ocean, swirled with fog, pounds into the steep sand slope that will disappear under the breakers of winter and re-form in its summer shape.

The guide stops frequently and gets everyone out to look at eiders bobbing offshore, or to put the telescope on gull colonies in the dunes, and the whimbrel and the marsh hawk and the least tern, who hovers above her egg in a small hollow in the sand. When the chick hatches, it must get up and run from its enemy, the scavenging gull. This is so chancy that the female tern is programed to lay more eggs that season, although she never learns to choose a safer nest.

All this the young guide discusses with the druggist and his wife and the two women who know nothing about birds, but don't let on. The Canadian birder knows it all, and much more. He won't even look at the least tern, whom he has "got" too

89

◄ Mill Pond, Sandwich

many times. Bird watching is almost as possessive as shooting. It's "I got him," "I took him." The bird does not exist until seen. He can name most of the multiple birds of Monomoy, before the guide, if possible. He has not, however, got the Hudsonian godwit for his Life List, and this is what he has come from Canada to seek.

A hundred and fifty years ago the lighthouse at the south end of the island was on the shore. Now it is a mile inland, because of the buildup of sand below it. From the light tower you can see deer drinking at a kettle pond, a muskrat scutting from the water to his hole, a group of birds guzzling in the marsh mud, and the top of the Canadian's head as he crouches behind a bush to catch a spotted sandpiper in molt.

The lighthouse is cleanly painted, the beds made up, the kitchen stocked with soup and beans. The two women want to stay here forever, or at least to eat lunch, but it's off to explore Powder Hole and the marshy feeding grounds that bring all the birds to Monomoy.

Migrating birds must go as far south of the equator as they go north. If they breed at 70° north, in the Tundra, they must winter in Argentina. Birds who have long journeys to make rest on Monomoy to store food, putting on three times their weight in body fat. Dowitchers, sewing-machine birds, snowy egrets like young ballet dancers, are going greedily at the mud, long beaks stabbing like pistons.

The guide calls a tern a turd by mistake, and blushes. And blushes again as he explains the sex life of the ticks, which can be seen lounging on the end of long grasses beside the path, like hitchhikers. A male tick can't tell a female until he bumps into her. He penetrates her anywhere, and she stores it for those long winter evenings when there is nothing on television, and then fertilizes herself.

Late in the day the visitors walk along the north end of the island, where the incoming tide covers all the swampy land. Everybody is soaking wet and covered with ticks and the bites of huge green flies. The Canadian has put an egg into the guide's shirt pocket, and then stumbled against him and smashed it. He still has not taken his godwit. He is sulking anyway, because he miscalled a ruddy turnstone in

90

Old windmill, Sandwich

Salt Pond inlet, Eastham ▶

spring plumage and the guide corrected him, to get his own back for the egg. The druggist and his wife are not speaking to each other, since they made bird noises at some bitterns in the bushes and discovered they were chirping at each other. The two women are tired and sit down with their backs to the telescope and refuse to look at the yellow-legged dowitcher.

"I've got him!" With a broken cry, the Canadian breaks into a clumsy gallop through the swamp, with his binoculars up to his eyes, and falls into a shallow pond.

"My lifer! My lifer!"

The Hudsonian godwit flies unconcerned a quarter of a mile away. Inshore, flocks of gulls, terns, and sanderlings wait for low tide, heads to the wind so as not to be blown over.

The sailor king appears out of the twilight, and the party wades to the boat without bothering to turn up trouser legs or take off shoes. Five minutes out to sea, the engine catches fire in clouds of blue smoke. George V, mortified, has to be towed in by a clam boat.

"Had a good day?" the rescuer calls back.

"You bet!" the Canadian shouts, his face still glowing with triumph. "I took my Hudsonian godwit!"

The godwit flies on to the south, and so do many of the people who have been part of the Cape Cod summer.

Suddenly in September everyone is gone. The best days are coming. Deeper colors, fresher air, a more urgent need to enjoy this beautiful land before it is too late.

Friends meet friends again—where has the summer gone, and the things they planned to do?—and start to plan all the things they never will do this winter.

West Falmouth harbor